NOSTALGIA PANAMERICANA

SELLING ROMANCE IN COLOR

EARLY MORNING TAKE-OFF OF PAN AMERICAN CLIPPER SHIP, MIAMI, FLORIDA   50

PHOTO BY GERECKE

Text and photography by W. Donald Thomas
Published in Dunedin, Florida, 1987

Artist's rendition of an
Aeromarine-Curtiss flying boat.
Scheduled service, late 1929,
New York to Atlantic City.

FRONT COVER — An early 1935 folder advertising "The World's Largest, Most Luxurious Airliners — The Clipper Ships." The Sikorsky S-42 is shown.

BACK COVER — Cover of large beautiful 1937 Trans Pacific brochure of PAA. "Beyond that sunset lies Cathay...," a thousand words describing the thrill of the flight to China across the Pacific. Included in this expensive piece of publicity was a large illuminated map of the Pacific routes, a large cutout picture of the interior of a Clipper, many photographs, and much descriptive text.

Copyright © 1987 by W. Donald Thomas

First Edition, 1987.
Library of Congress No. 87-90148
ISBN No. 0-9618642-0-6
Manufactured in Singapore

FOREWORD

By R.E.G. Davies

IN SPITE of the modest disclaimer in his introduction, Don Thomas's book can take its place in the annals of history with as much justification as some of the scholarly works that adorn library bookshelves. These are consulted for reference and enlightenment but seldom perused for pleasure. I guarantee that this book will not be consigned to such a fate.

Not that this is yet another so-called "coffee-table" production. This is no mere collection of photographs, randomly selected, loosely assembled, and with a few often misleading captions. Don Thomas gets to the grass roots of Pan American Airways through publicity literature which is totally evocative of the era of the flying boats, when to travel by air was still an adventure. And there are a few welcome bonus items at the end of the book.

For all Don's protestations to the contrary, his book has as much a place in the airline bibliography of Pan Am as do learned tomes such as Bender and Altschul's **Chosen Instrument,** or Richard Daley's **An American Saga,** or Wes Newton's **A Perilous Sky.** While the latter tell us, in considerable detail, the fascinating stories of intrigue, corporate maneuvring, and international diplomacy that built the airline. Don's colorful selection of memorabilia tells us what it was like for the airline traveller even to think about the idea of taking an air trip in the 1930s. And after all, the passenger was the customer, the consumer, the reason why Pan American Airways was brought into being in the first place, and the reason for its continued existence.

"Flying Down to Rio" was a phrase used in the formative years of commercial aviation in America to evoke the spirit of adventure and romance of air travel. This book recaptures the glorious mood of expectation that prevailed during that period. However, Don correctly reminds us that to take a flying boat cruise that included three days in Rio would have cost $865 — about $10,000 in today's currency. Seven days would have cost only $30 more, a neat reflection on relative values at that time. Today, the seven days would cost almost as much as the air fare.

These colorful pictures portray "The Land of Enchantment" (not to mention the "Fright Service!") as no scholarly work can do. Such an approach complements the work of the professional historian and is no less important. And as Don states, the artists impressions of the aircraft and the environment in which they operated make their mark as indelibly as photographs.

I heartily recommend this book to all true lovers of aviation history. It is a joy to the eye and truly mirrors an almost forgotten era when airline pioneering was exciting and wonderful, matched only by the colorful literature that promoted it.

Ron Davies is Curator of Air Transport at the National Air & Space Museum, Smithsonian Institution, Washington, D.C., and is acknowledged as the world authority on aviation history. His books: "History of the World's Airlines," "Airlines of the United States Since 1914," and "Airlines of Latin America Since 1919" are universally regarded as the "bibles" of aviation history.

NOSTALGIA PANAMERICANA

T HIS BOOK is in no way a history of an airline or airlines. Its purpose is to show the color and artistic beauty of the old brochures, timetables, and baggage labels of Pan American Airways and other airlines of the Americas which used flying boats in the 1920's and 1930's. The flying boat mostly passed into history when superseded by longer-range landplanes which could carry more passengers and cargo at far less cost for fuel.

Several good books have been written on the history of Pan American Airways and dozens about other airlines, complete with photographs of aircraft and personnel, but usually in black and white. There is thus no need to repeat the history or the photographs, as this has been done very well by many authors. However, the art work, the colorful promotion efforts, especially by Pan American Airways in the golden age of airline expansion, is worthy of being reproduced in original blazing colors. A minimum of research was needed for this volume — the data is mostly right from the brochures. Some items are reduced in size to fit the pages.

Pan American's artists and publicity department gave us a priceless legacy of historic material of the flying boat era, and all in living color. Pan American was selling romance, not just seats on its aircraft. Nowadays much of such commercial artwork has been replaced by photography. To some of us old-timers, photographs of jet aircraft lack some of the appeal of an artist's depiction of a flying boat.

Accompanying these usually rare items are quotations from within them, which give an insight into the accomplishments of the pioneers in the early days of aviation and the efforts of the airlines to convince the public of the advantages and safety of flying.

These items are scarce and seldom seen nowadays. Who saved old time-tables and brochures? Who saves them now? An outdated timetable is a danger — it is thrown out as soon as it is replaced with an up-to-date one. No tour agency wanted to be swamped with outdated travel publicity. Most airlines don't even remember what they used a few years previously, and seldom saved anything, even if the airline survived into the present day. Many did not themselves survive. Even a few packrats like the Author would pick up only one copy of a Zeppelin timetable when they were free by the dozen on tour agency racks in the 1930's. Now they are eagerly sought after but seldom encountered. There is much airline history in these timetables and other publicity and I'd like to share it. These are all from my collection, and I am always looking for more.

1914

On January 1, 1914, pilot Tony Jannus took off for a 23 minute flight from St. Petersburg to Tampa, Florida. This was the start of the first scheduled airline in the world, the St. Petersburg-Tampa Airboat Line.

St. Petersburg-Tampa
AIRBOAT LINE

Fast Passenger and Express Service

SCHEDULE:

Lv. St. Petersburg	10:00 A.M.
Arrive Tampa	10:30 A.M.
Leave Tampa	11:00 A.M.
Ar. St. Petersburg	11:30 A.M.
Lv. St. Petersburg	2:00 P.M.
Arrive Tampa	2:30 P.M.
Leave Tampa	3:00 P.M.
Ar. St. Petersburg	3:30 P.M.

Special Flight Trips

Can be arranged through any of our agents or by communicating directly with the St. Petersburg Hangar. Trips covering any distance over all-water routes and from the waters' surface to several thousand feet high AT PAS—SENGERS' REQUEST.

A minimum charge of $15 per Special Flight.

Rates: $5.00 Per Trip.   **Round Trip $10.**   **Booking for Passage in Advance.**

NOTE--Passengers are allowed a weight of 200 pounds GROSS including hand baggage, excess charged at $5.00 per 100 pounds, minimum charge 25 cents. EXPRESS RATES, for packages, suit cases, mail matter, etc., $5.00 per hundred pounds, minimum charge 25 cents. Express carried from hangar to hangar only, delivery and receipt by shipper.

Tickets on Sale at Hangars or

CITY NEWS STAND
F. C. WEST, Prop.

271 CENTRAL AVENUE   ST. PETERSBURG, FLORIDA

Replica of the original Benoist airboat, built by the Florida Aviation Historical Society, which re-enacted the flight on its 70th anniversary, January 1, 1984.
Photo by Margaret Deaton.

1921

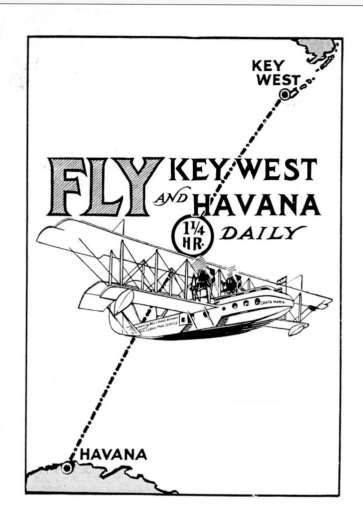

The first regular international passenger service from the U.S.

Twice a day flights between Key West and Havana.

A boon to thirsty travelers in the days of prohibition.

Questions inside this brochure:

"Can passengers carry baggage?" (The answer was "Yes — 30 lbs") "Your heavy baggage follows the same night by steamer."

"Is this really an event to look forward to?" (The answer was "Yes, no advance in transportation on this hemisphere has been so eventful. Once by flying boat from Key West to Havana you will say "Never again by steamer.")

Above, only known surviving copy of Aeromarine West Indies Airways baggage label. Removed from an old suitcase. Original color, light blue.

1922-1923

Aeromarine Airways took over the assets and routes of Aeromarine West Indies Airways and boasted of 6 "Flying Cruisers" (2 engines) which could carry 11 passengers, and 7 "Flying Boats" (single engine) which could carry 5 passengers.

"Passengers wear their ordinary clothes. No leather garments, goggles or other paraphernalia are necessary in Aeromarine Cruisers!" (This apparently didn't apply to the open-cockpit flying boats.)

"Dainty buffet lunches" are served in the beautiful mahogany cabin of the eleven-passenger Aeromarine flying cruisers on special charter flights." (Apparently no eats on the smaller craft.)

Note that St. Petersburg and Bellaire Heights are listed on the front of the brochure, but inside it says: "St. Petersburg-Bellaire Heights, rate on application."

"Minimum sightseeing flight — $5.00 per passenger." (Not bad.)

Colorful baggage label, designed by Public Relations Director Harry Bruno in Sloppy Joe's famous bar in Havana. Although thousands were printed, they are now unobtainable.

FLY
Aeromarine
FLYING BOAT SERVICE

Key West—Havana
Palm Beach — Miami — Bimini
Nassau—Tampa
St. Petersburg—Belleair Heights

AEROMARINE AIRWAYS, Inc.
C. F. REDDEN, PRESIDENT
Executive Offices, Times Building, New York City

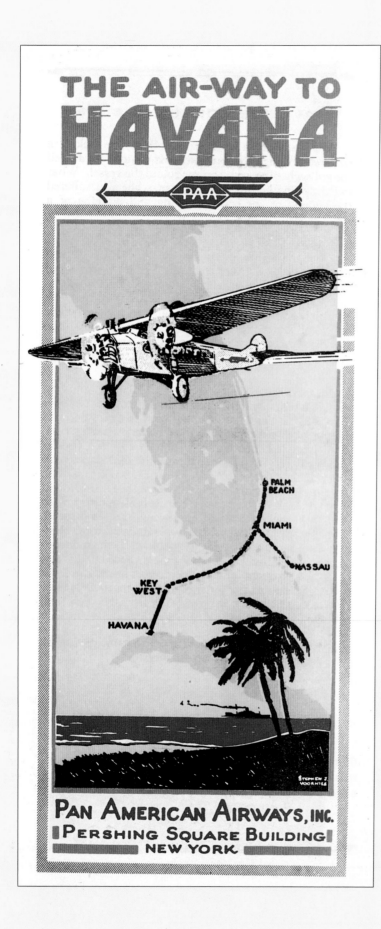

THE AIR-WAY TO HAVANA

PAA

PALM BEACH

MIAMI

NASSAU

KEY WEST

HAVANA

PAN AMERICAN AIRWAYS, INC.
PERSHING SQUARE BUILDING
NEW YORK

PAN AMERICAN AIRWAYS, Inc., first timetable, January 1928.

Mail service between Key West and Havana had been maintained since October, 1927. Now, in January, 1928, daily passenger service was inaugurated with 8-passenger Fokker planes.

This timetable was reprinted in 1967 for Pan Am's 40th Anniversary and in 1977 for its 50th.

Excerpts from this brochure:

"How many times have you stood on the deck of a steamer, tossing in a rough sea and enviously watched the gulls wheeling and dipping 'round the vessel. What swiftness and lightness, what ease, while you suffered the agonies of the endless rolling and pitching of a spiteful sea. How you longed for the smooth, quick flight of the gull." Then follows a pitch for "the comfort, speed and safety of aerial transportation."

The next timetable from PAA was a reprinting of the same cover, surcharged "New Schedule. Effective Sept. 15, 1928 to Dec. 15, 1928." The inside was different, now outlining plans for passengers to be carried immediately from PAA's new hangar at Miami to Havana via Key West, and, starting December 15th, direct service from Miami to Havana.

1929

This flight schedule, on cardboard stock, is from 1929, and gives complete schedules as far south as Trinidad "over the Lindbergh Circle route."

Only mail was carried on the Central American routes, but "passenger service over these routes will be inaugurated as rapidly as every detail for the comfort and safety of passengers is completed," it says.

8-passenger Sikorsky S-38 amphibians were operated on this West Indies route, in addition to the Fokker landplanes flying to Havana.

Col. Charles Lindbergh surveyed these circular Caribbean routes for PAA with the "Spirit of St. Louis" and an S-38 in 1929.

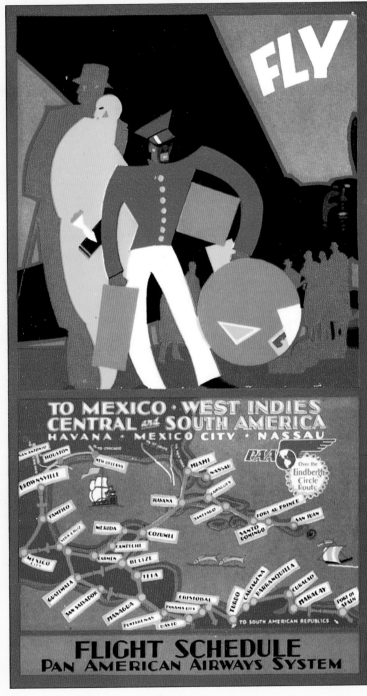

Baggage sticker listing all the West Indies and Central American countries on the Lindbergh Circle.

1929

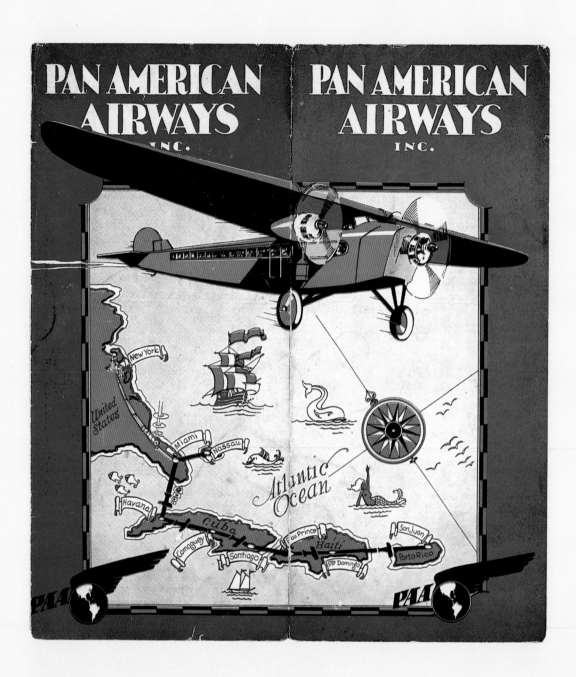

This colorful 1929 brochure gives schedules on the back cover for through Rail-Air service from New York, Chicago, St. Louis and other midwest cities to Miami and thence to Havana, Nassau, and on to the West Indies, using the new Fokker F-10 trimotors.

Inside, however, the language could only be described as flowery:

"South with the birds"...."over the smooth highway of the air in comfort and safety, modern travelers follow the birds to Cuba and the tropical Indies!"

"Over the Violet Sea...." the airliner glides slowly forward over the ground, gathers momentum — and one realizes, half incredulously, that he is flying..."

"Speeding to Happiness"...."Pan American airliners, moving in comfortable haste, cut hours and even days from travel time...."

"Magic sails"...."Airliners of the Pan American fleet are all twelve-passenger tri-motored cabin monoplanes"...."All mail, luggage, and passengers are weighed....Steward service, complete toilet facilities, running water, full vision windows, commodious lounge chairs...."

(Do we have better nowadays on the jets?)

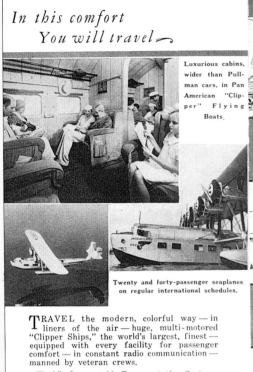

To the Spanish Main — by Commodore or S-40. (There were three S-40s and 14 Commodores in PAA's fleet)

To the Mid-Pacific — by Martin M-130 China Clipper. (There were three of these China Clipper types in PAA's fleet).

1932

August 15, 1932 schedule

PAA postcard

THE SIKORSKY S-40

Often called "a collection of spare parts flying in formation."

Actually the three S-40s were the largest civil aircraft in service at that time. Each carried 40 passengers on Caribbean and Latin American routes.

These were the first Pan American planes to be called "Clippers" which became a company trademark.

Train from New York to Miami,
Atlantic Coast Line.

Plane from Miami to San Juan, "Porto Rico,"
Pan American Airways.

Steamer from San Juan to New York,
the SS COAMO of the **Porto Rico Line.**

Inside paragraphs:

"The First Air Cruise!"
"Into a New World"
"Cocktail Time in Havana"
"Santiago-San Juan Hill-Guantanamo"
"Mysterious Haiti!"
"Into the Domain of Christophe"
"The Land of Columbus"
"Porto Rico — Medley of Colors"
"Coamo Springs — In a Miniature Switzerland"
"And so to Sea!"

The Map inside:

"Over the Lindbergh Circle"

(It was years later before the official
spelling of Puerto Rico was changed to
conform to the desires of its people.)

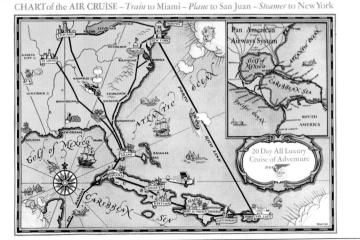

CHART of the AIR CRUISE ~ *Train* to Miami ~ *Plane* to San Juan ~ *Steamer* to New York

Colorful train-plane folder of 1930.

THE WORLD'S GREATEST AIR TRANSPORTATION SYSTEM

Links the United States with
32 Latin American Countries

FACTS
about
PAN AMERICAN

The following figures are for
the period from January 1,
1929, to November 1, 1930

101	Modern Airliners
80	Pilots, each with more than 2000 hours' experience
89	Modern airports
42	Operating ground radio stations
19,190	Miles of airways
100,000	Miles flown weekly
100	Miles per hour average speed for passengers, mail and express
6,039,645	Miles flown to date
36,007	Passengers carried to date
1,025,000	Pounds of baggage carried to date
1,227,292	Pounds of mail carried to date
1,600	People employed

Constant two-way radio communication between all airliners and ground stations.

THE WORLD'S GREATEST AIR TRANSPORTATION SYSTEM

12 Railroads were listed as associated with the "Plane-Train" of PAA. The inside of this 13-page 1930 folder used the same rainbow colors as the cover. Samples above and at right.

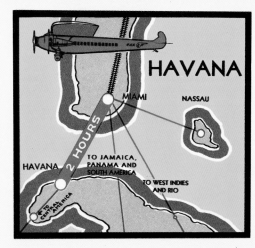

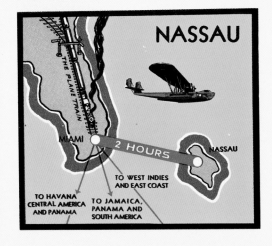

1935

Pre-World War II —
The S-42 Clippers.

Inside

Another colorful brochure featuring the S-42 Clipper. A total of 10 of these Sikorskys were used by Pan American before they were superseded by landplanes.

Departure tax from Nassau was 50¢. (Now its $5.00)

At left, an artist's rendering of a sleek-looking S-42.

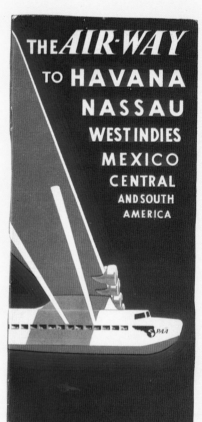

The AIR-WAY

"WINGS OVER THE AMERICAS"....
(Early 1930s brochure)

Below, a peek at the inside.

Similar colorful pages for:
NASSAU AND JAMAICA
WEST INDIES
MEXICO CITY-MERIDA
CENTRAL AMERICA and PANAMA
SOUTH AMERICA

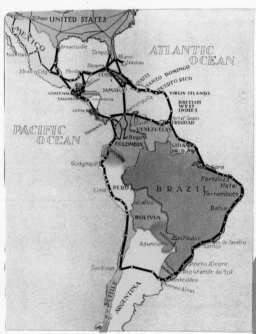

Here Is the New World of Travel Wonders

A LIVING map in full life size unrolls for your delighted gaze along America's international airways. Take your choice of 100 colorful cities in 33 glamorous countries. Cruise over them in the restful ease of a great airliner. See every mountain and river and forest in their natural colors and their true relationship to the entire picture. Then land . . . anywhere on the 26,652 miles of the airways . . . and explore the intimate details that give the amazing picture its meaning. This is the *new idea* in travel that has brought delight to 200,000 travelers over the Pan American Airways System.

America's finest trains or swiftest airlines will take you southward, on through tickets from your home city direct to Miami or Tampa, or to Brownsville, Texas, the great international gateways, whence giant "Clipper Ships of the Air" will bear you to any country of the Caribbean in two and one-half days, to the most "distant" capital of South America in seven short days!

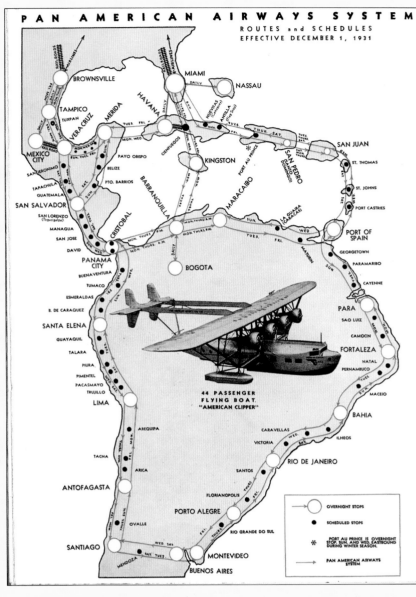

"SHORTEST TIME TO SUNSHINE.."

The inside of a PAA 1931 brochure, shown at left, was often used in Pan American's timetables, annual reports, and advertising in the early 1930s.

The S-40 is pictured in the center. It was a workhorse on the Caribbean routes but was never used on the long haul to Buenos Aires.

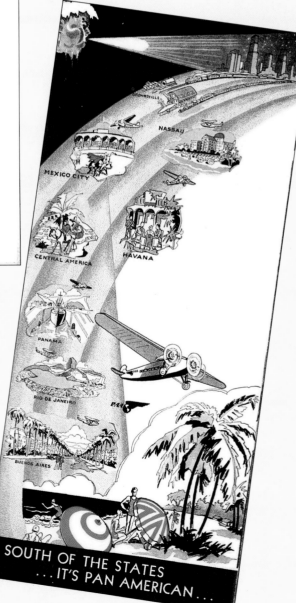

The back cover of this brochure, at right, shows the tri-motored Fokkers which were the first aircraft types operated by the infant Pan American Airways, Inc., on the airway from Miami and Key West to Havana.

A 1936 brochure — the S-42 again.

"Flying the Lindbergh Circle — 7777 magic miles around the Caribbean Sea — the West Indies, South America and Mexico — in a ten days holiday!"

From page 2 of brochure.

**Clipper Cruises Are New Sensation
—Hit of Year in Travel World**

Smart Travelers — This Year — Are Going by Air on Swift
Flights to Colorful, Romantic Isles of the Caribbean—
Luxury Airliners Offer Traveler Opportunity of Life-
time—"Abroad" and Back Again Within a Week

By Virginia Sentner

CHICAGO—The latest thing in the everlasting adventure of travel—
Clipper Cruises to the romantic isles of the Caribbean—have just been
announced for the coming travel season. Here is news that appeals to

12-day cruise (3 days in Rio) was $865.

19-day cruise (10 days in Rio) was $895. All expenses.

"10 countries along the way, 10,000 sights and sounds and experiences."

Below: Interior view of the S-42, part of this big 14-page brochure.

1934

In the 1930s the S-40 was pictured on labels of Pan American Airways and Panair do Brasil. Passengers were on the loading dock. Similar labels were printed showing the tri-motor landplanes of PAA used by MEXICANA and PANAGRA. The Author has not yet located a copy of the identical PANAGRA label. Does anyone have one?

18:—"Off to Havana" on one of Pan American Airways Clipper Ships, Miami, Florida.

PHOTO BY G. W. ROMER.

An S-40 at dock, Dinner Key, Miami. Sikorsky made three of this type for PAA, before it was replaced by the streamlined S-42.

Flying Clipper Cruises AROUND SOUTH AMERICA

FEB 16 1940

PAA PAN AMERICAN AIRWAYS

February, 1940, brochure.

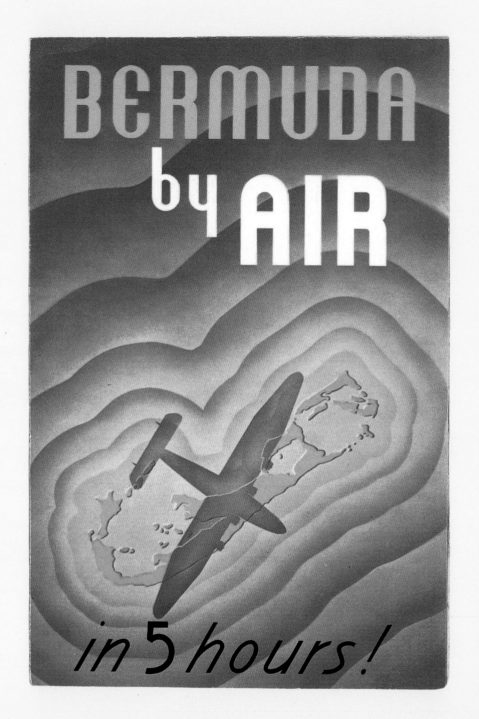

In June 1937, a joint service to Bermuda was inaugurated by Pan American Airways and Imperial Airways (Bermuda), Ltd. PAA used an S-42 renamed "Bermuda Clipper." Imperial used the RMA "Cavalier," a Short S-23 Empire flying boat.

In January, 1939, the "Cavalier" was forced down in the Atlantic by icing and was lost. PAA continued the run with reduced schedules, using the "Bermuda Clipper."

Baggage label, RMA Cavalier.

1939

Following the opening, in the summer of 1939, of transatlantic services to Europe, in December the Boeing 314 transatlantic Clippers provided flights to Bermuda from New York for $40, one-way, enroute to Lisbon, Portugal. This golden brochure was in use while the Clippers were still using Port Washington, L.I., but it said "from North Beach Airport when opened." That would be the new Marine Air Terminal at LaGuardia.

Pan American used this baggage label on Bermuda flights in the 1940's.

This ticket envelope was used in the 1940's.

1942

WINGS OF DEMOCRACY

No. 3   JULY 15, 1942

Weekly pamphlets were issued by PAA starting in July, 1942, telling of the ongoing efforts of Pan American in furthering the war effort. Weekly stories entitled "Clippers at Work," "Making Way for War," "Pacific Clippers in Wartime," "Somewhere in Africa," etc., described PAA's wartime activities.

In wartime the big Boeing Clippers were painted gray and used for priority cargo and passengers only, shuttling back and forth across the Atlantic and Pacific on a continuous basis.

Airmail sticker

B-314 Clipper at Dinner Key seaplane base, Miami, 1942.

1945

One of American Export Airlines' "Flying Aces"　　　*LaGuardia Field*

Postcard of VS-44A mailed Oct. 1, 1945. American Export Airlines was granted a certificate for wartime Transatlantic service to Ireland in early 1942. The first VS-44A, "Excalibur" was lost in a crash in 1942. The other two, Exeter and Excambion, maintained transatlantic service for the Naval Air Transport Service for the war's duration.

Inside of May 1, 1945, postwar schedule of Am. Export. The line was merged into American Overseas Airlines in late 1945. The flying boats were sold. Pan American Airways eventually controlled the airline.

TRANSATLANTIC AIR SERVICE
1945 Summer Schedule
U. S. A. — Newfoundland — Eire — England and connections beyond
Service operated with The Famous Four-Engine "Flying Aces"

MILES	GREENWICH TIME	LOCAL TIME	*3 ROUND TRIPS WEEKLY		LOCAL TIME	GREENWICH TIME	MILES
0000	1200	8:00 A. M.	Dep. . . . NEW YORK, N. Y., LaGuardia Field . . . . Arr. (Marine Terminal)		2:45 P. M.	1845	3502
1111	1915	4:45 P. M.	Arr. } . . . . BOTWOOD, NEWFOUNDLAND . . . . { Dep.		9:00 A. M.	1130	2391
	2100	6:30 P. M.	Dep. {	{ Arr.	7:15 A. M.	0945	
3112	0830	9:30 A. M.	Arr. . . . . . FOYNES, EIRE (Shannon Airport) . . . . Dep.		8:00 P. M.	1900	0390
3502	Direct Connection by British Overseas Airways. Flight Time 2½ hours.		{	FOYNES, EIRE LONDON, ENGLAND (Airways House)	}	Direct Connection by British Overseas Airways. Flight Time 2½ hours.	0390
							0000

CONNECTIONS TO CONTINENTAL EUROPE, SCANDINAVIAN COUNTRIES AND MEDITERRANEAN AREA UPON APPLICATION

Schedules shown above are not guaranteed, and are subject to change without notice.
*Departures from New York, Tuesdays, Thursdays and Saturdays: From Foynes, Wednesdays, Fridays and Sundays.

Baggage label

1939

The 1939 TransPacific timetable of Pan American Airways System. The Big Boeing 314, already in North Atlantic service, was now in use from San Francisco to Hong Kong.

Baggage labels like the one at right were used for Atlantic Service, Bermuda Service, Alaska Service, and in Latin America.

1941

The AIR TRAVELER booklets contained much information on the countries covered, as well as a wealth of advertising. This CUBA one is dated 1941. The AIR TRAVELER in the PACIFIC was 1940; the AIR TRAVELER in PORT was dated 1939, but different booklets were published by two publishers. The West Indies edition showed an S-42 Sikorsky flying boat on the cover, and the Central America one pictured a DC-3.

1950's

In 1950 PAN AMERICAN AIRWAYS became PAN AMERICAN WORLD AIRWAYS.

A series of seven labels covering the Pacific services was printed: ALASKA, HAWAII, ORIENT, PHILIPPINES, AUSTRALIA, USA and NEW ZEALAND.

Brochures and a colourful assortment of baggage and propaganda labels in the 1950s continued with the traditional fine art work of PAA.

1930's

PAN AMERICAN LINES!!
NEW YORK to MIAMI!!

Red and blue — beautiful!

———————

Relax — it's NOT PAA —
It's a BUS schedule!

SCHEDULED AIRMAIL AND PASSENGER SERVICE

SERVICIO AEREO DE CORREO Y PASAJEROS

Habana - Cienfuegos - Sta. Clara - Morón - Camagüey - Manzanillo - Bayamo - Santiago - Antilla - Cayo Mambí - Baracoa - Guantánamo - Nueva Gerona

COMPAÑIA NACIONAL CUBANA DE AVIACION CURTISS   COMPAÑIA NACIONAL CUBANA DE AVIACION CURTISS

Cia Nacional Cubana de Aviacion Curtiss started in 1929. In 1932 it was bought by Pan American Airways and the Curtiss name was dropped.

A Curtiss trimotor Ford is shown at Havana Airport, loading passengers.

A 1946 schedule of Cubana is shown at left. Pan American World Airways divested itself of the last of its Cubana stock in 1954.

After Pan American took over the airline, the name CURTISS was cut off the bottom of this label for use by CNCA.

1934

Printed in Lima, Peru, this 1934 timetable shows an artist's conception of a PAA flying boat.

Actually, the Commodores used on the route to Rio and Buenos Aires in 1934 had twin tail-fins. This year of 1934 was the year that the Sikorsky S-42 took over the route to Rio and B.A. from the Commodores. The S-42 also had twin tail-fins, and the triple-tailed Boeing 314, not introduced into Transatlantic service until 1939, was never used in regular scheduled Latin-American service.

Inside it says "Las Grandes Distancias Ya No Existen" (Long distances no longer exist").

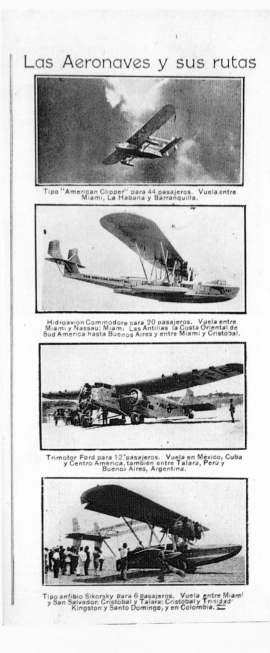

At right, the four main aircraft types used by PAA in Latin America in 1934, before the addition of the S-42 and the other landplanes beside the Ford.

Illustration at right is from the inside of above timetable.

1929

The color used mostly in their advertising by the Grace steamship and chemical interests was green — note the green background on this colorful brochure. The plane is a Ford Tri-Motor.

The first two baggage labels of PANAGRA are shown above. There is an interesting story about them. The author had a letter from General Harris in Massachusetts asking for a photo of the P.A.G.A.I. label. He wrote that when he first organized the airline in Lima he had no information on just what the new airline was to be called. So on the first labels he used the initials of the airline, P.A.G.A.I. Finally Harris received word from the head office in New York that the name of the airline was to be PANAGRA, so he re-designed the label. Both varieties are now rare.

1939

A 1939 leaflet from PANAGRA

"Coast-to-coast in 5½ hours" was from Santiago, Chile, to Buenos Aires, in DC-3s.

"PANAGRA planes have crossed the Andes more than 3,522 times up to January 1939," it says.

The Germans meanwhile had organized a thru route from Europe to the West Coast. DEUTSCHE LUFTHANSA flew over the South Atlantic to Brazil. CONDOR flew across Mato Grosso to the Bolivian border, LAB flew to LaPaz, Bolivia, and LUFTHANSA PERU connected at LaPaz to fly into Lima. Then SEDTA of Ecuador could connect to SCADTA in Colombia to complete the coverage.

THE GERMAN CONNECTION

All these airlines were connected with the German company, although PAA had purchased control of SCADTA in 1930.

PAN AMERICAN
AIRWAYS SYSTEM

11 HORAS
HOURS

AGENTES
CIA. DE AVIACION
PAN AMERICAN ARGENTINA, S. A.
AV. R. SAENZ PEÑA 612   BUENOS AIRES
U. T. 33, Av. 1800-8713-2492

BUENOS AIRES-RIO

This colorful folder is from Buenos Aires. It is a good view of the Sikorsky S-42, used by PAA on the run from Miami to Rio and Buenos Aires after 1934, replacing the Commodores.

SISTEMA AEREO PAN AMERICAN AIRWAYS

HORARIOS-TARIFAS
PAA
EN VIGOR DESDE AGOSTO 1, 1934

SISTEMA AEREO PAN AMERICAN AIRWAYS

PASAJEROS CORREO-EXPRESS

HORARIOS-TARIFAS
PAA
EN VIGOR DESDE JULIO 4, 1935

These small timetables, for Mexico, Central America and Havana only, from 1934 and 1935, show an artist's conception of PAA flying boats and land planes; the latter no doubt a DC-2.

Stationery folder given to PANAIR passengers in Brazil.

Passengers are shown deplaning from a Commodore flying boat, one of the 14 which Pan American received when it took over New York Rio & Buenos Aires Line in 1930.

1939

Despite the S-42 pictured on timetable at left, only Pan American Airways used this aircraft for their flights through Brazil. Panair do Brasil used the luxurious Commodores and the smaller S-38s, later getting some S-43s and PBY Catalinas.

At right, Lockheed Electras (as shown), Lodestars, and Constellations were used by PANAIR in later years, after the flying boats were scrapped. Also used were DC-2s, DC-3s, DC-6As, DC-7Cs, and Caravelles.

Airmail label

1943

Below, from the inside of a 1943 folder in Portuguese, printed in Rio de Janeiro. All these aircraft were used by Panair do Brasil except the bottom three on right and the S-42 on left; these were Pan American Airways.

OS "COMMODORES" · Os veteranos "Commodores", hydro-aviões de grande solidez, capacidade e conforto, proprios para vôos maritimos de cabotagem, são monoplanos de grande envergadura, equipados com dois motores. Foram utilizados em todas as linhas littoraneas, assim como na linha Belém-Manáos, trafegando actualmente na linha costeira entre o Recife e Belém do Pará, servindo todos os portos intermediarios.

OS "AMERICAN CLIPPERS" (S-40) · Com a construcção destes apparelhos, iniciou-se em 1931 a phase da utilização dos grandes hydro-aviões nas linhas aereas regulares, por iniciativa da Pan American Airways. O "American Clipper" é um amphibio de grandes dimensões, equipado com 4 motores. O seu conforto, a segurança de suas operações e a sua velocidade marcaram novos rumos á aviação commercial moderna.

OS "BRAZILIAN CLIPPERS" (S-42) · Essas aeronaves já não foram mais amphibias, mas hydro-aviões, com capacidade para 32 passageiros em percursos mais longos e em condições excepcionaes de conforto, alem de grande velocidade. Os "S-42" são equipados com quatro motores. Essas aeronaves trafegam entre o Rio de Janeiro e Miami, nos Estados Unidos, entre New York e as Bermudas, assim como em outras aerovias.

OS "BABY-CLIPPERS" (S-43) · São amphibios Sikorsky, de alta velocidade, destinados aos serviços costeiros rapidos. São utilizados nas linhas da Panair ao longo das costas brasileiras. Bi-motores confortaveis para 15 passageiros, esses apparelhos incorporam todos os aperfeiçôamentos dos grandes "Clippers", accrescidos da facilidade de manobras nos numerosos portos intermediarios em que escalam.

OS "FAIRCHILDS" · Este tipo de apparelho é um monoplano, amphibio e monomotor, caracterizado pela sua robustez, estabilidade de vôo e velocidade, tendo sido construido, sob encommenda da Panair, especialmente para os serviços da linha amazonica entre Belém, Manáos e Porto Velho. Pertence a um modelo recente e adequado ao vôo sobre regiões como a Amazonia, onde faz numerosas escalas intermediarias.

OS "LOCKHEED · ELECTRAS" · São apparelhos monoplanos, bi-motores, inteiramente metallicos, utilizados na costa occidental do Mexico, em Cuba, no Territorio do Alaska e na Rêde Aeroviaria Mineira da Panair. Rapidos e confortaveis, os "Electras" são um dos typos mais efficientes do mundo, motivo pelo qual foram adquiridos por quasi todas as grandes companhias de navegação aerea da Europa e outros continentes.

OS "DOUGLAS D-C 3" · Aviões de grandes dimensões, os "Douglas" incorporam em sua construcção numerosos aperfeiçôamentos que os tornam o apparelho mais veloz e mais confortavel do mundo em seu typo. São monoplanos de dois motores, utilizados nas linhas: Rio - Porto Alegre - Buenos Aires e Rio - São Paulo - Curityba - Foz do Iguassú - Assumpção - Buenos Aires, na transandina e ao longo da costa do Pacifico.

OS "CHINA CLIPPERS" · São grandes monoplanos com poltronas e leitos confortaveis para viagens longas, de dia e de noite. Foi com este typo que a Pan American Airways inaugurou a sua linha transpacifica de passageiros em Novembro de 1935, vencendo em 4 dias e meio mais de 13.000 kilometros de distancia entre a California e a China, no maior percurso transoceanico existente no mundo inteiro.

OS "CLIPPERS OCEANICOS" · Desenvolvimento dos typos anteriores de "Clippers", mas com as dimensões e performances consideravelmente augmentadas, os "Clippers Oceanicos", recem-construidos, são a ultima palavra em materia de hydro-aviões de grande potencia e capacidade. São utilizados pela Pan American Airways nas suas linhas oceanicas do Atlantico e do Pacifico, approximando a America da Europa e da Asia.

OS "BOEINGS SUB - STRATOSPHERICOS" · Sob a designação de "Boeing-307", a Fabrica Boeing construiu para a Pan American Airways esses grandes aviões destinados ao vôo nas altas camadas da atmosphera e a grande velocidade. São monoplanos metallicos de fuselagem circular hermeticamente fechada. Essas aeronaves entrarão brevemente em trafego nas principaes aerovias internacionaes do Systema P. A. A.

Above: Blotters used by NYRBA in advertising.

With these Commodore flying boats NYRBA operated a 7800 mile route from the U.S. to Buenos Aires in 1929-1930 before it was forced to sell out to Pan American Airways because it lacked a U.S. mail contract. Despite NYRBA's experience on the route with these largest and most luxurious flying boats in operation at the time, Pan American was designated as the U.S. government's "chosen instrument" in international aviation, and thus acquired the route and the aircraft.

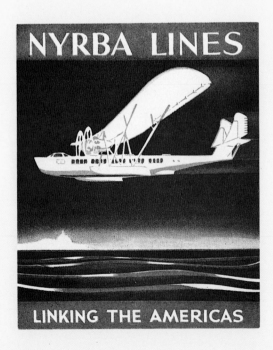

These blue and white baggage labels came in English, Spanish and Portuguese.

The top and bottom were cut off and used temporarily on the Commodores by PAA after their takeover of NYRBA.

1930

BY THE ROUTE OF THE SEA-GOING AIRLINERS

To the Land of Enchantment > > >

Magic cities, lands of rare enchantment . . . those "someday" ideals . . . are
brought within reach of the vacationist ~~the 's~~
~~giant ai~~ ~~Rio de Janei~~

day's time and distance. Over this 10,000 mile
system of modern airways, endless days aboard
slow-m~~~~rs are ch~~~~ like

AGENCIA BEST. B. AIRES

A Commodore with three engines?

Yes, its not wholly an artist's dream. The original
Consolidated type really had three engines, but due
to aerodynamic problems the top one was eliminated,
and NYRBA's Commodores were produced with two
engines.

NYRBA LINE was originally named TRIMOTOR
SAFETY AIRWAYS.

Two types of the rare label above were used
in Buenos Aires, although the NYRBA
office there must have been aware that
their Commodores had only two engines.

Ford Tri-Motors were
used on flights over
the Andes to
Santiago, Chile.

1941

July, 1941, schedule

$29 round trip from Miami to either Havana or Nassau.

This was the fare on July 1, 1941. However, this brochure said that these excursion fares were only good during the summer season — April 15 to December 19th.

The stylized DC-3 shows up well against the red background. On the flag above, Clipper flying boats are circling the earth.

PAA baggage label.

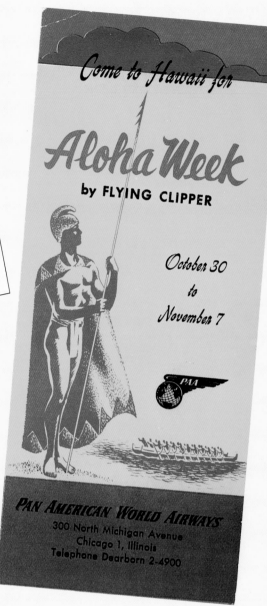

The liberal use of yellows, reds, and other colors made the advertisements of Pan American and its subsidiaries most attractive.

1930

A Pan American Airways subsidiary of 1930. The airline used a trimotor Ford, a Fokker F-10, and a Sikorsky S-38.

Service was later extended to Baltimore and Washington.

Sold to Eastern Air Transport in 1931.

This August 1931 timetable shows how Pan American teamed up with Boston-Maine Airways to offer joint daily passenger service from Boston to Maine points.

Tri-weekly passenger service was offered by PAA from Boston to Halifax via Portland, Bangor, Calais and St. John.

Reason for this service was to give PAA the experience of flying in northern conditions in preparation for proposed Transatlantic operations. Service was soon discontinued.

Boston-Maine baggage label shows their Stinson

1931

SCADTA's Dornier-Wal Colombia was featured in SCADTA publicity because of its graceful lines, although it could not be used up the Magdalena river, one of the main routes where floatplanes were used.

This colorful brochure is from 1931. Pan American Airways secretly owned a controlling interest in SCATDA by this time.

The German personnel were replaced with Americans in 1940, and the airline was renamed AVIANCA.

Baggage label

"Fright service" is offered. Most early airlines were not so honest.

This old 1927 poster of SCADTA was discovered in the AVIANCA files in 1944. It shows three types of aircraft SCADTA used on the rivers and harbors of Colombia in the 1920s: the Dornier Wal, the Dornier Merkur and the Junkers-F13.

1933

Ed.. C.-4-33-5000

The flying boat "Atlantico", one of the Dornier-Wals used by CONDOR for coastwise flying in Brazil. This schedule, Rio to Natal, north-bound, and Rio to Porto Alegre to the south, is from1933.

Compliments

"The future of Brazil depends on its communications" — "Save time and money, by using Serviço Aereo Condor"; another 1933 leaflet.

The Graf Zeppelin, making regular trips from Germany to Brazil at this time, used Condor as its South American agent.

Baggage label

1935-1937

This 1935 listing of passenger tariffs of CONDOR between Natal, Rio de Janeiro and Buenos Aires shows a panorama of Rio harbor with floatplanes landing and taking off, with the CONDOR launch heading for shore.

These trimotored floatplanes were versions of the German Junkers-52/3m. CONDOR had more than a dozen of them.

The 1937 timetable at right lists departures from Frankfurt, Germany, via Seville, Las Palmas and Bathurst to Natal. From Natal schedules are listed for 26 Brazilian cities, from Belém in the north and Buenos Aires, Argentina in the south. The Mato Grosso-Bolivia route lists 10 cities, from São Paulo to Cuyabá. From the Mato Grosso city of Corumbá, Lloyd Aereo Boliviano stops at five cities on the way to La Paz.

Airmail labels

1927

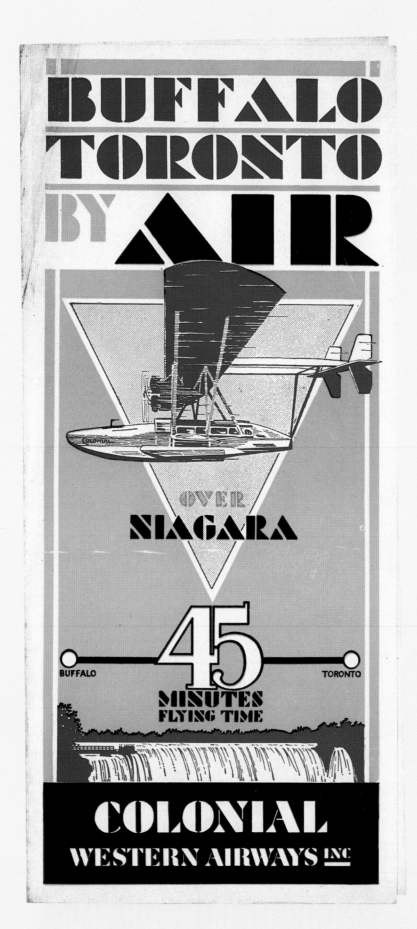

"Forty-five minutes of inspiring flight between Buffalo and Toronto!"

"A pilot and reserve pilot accompany each ship." (I'm glad).

"...Your huge plane approaches — the falls are marked in the distance — then you come nearer! And now the plane swings slowly in a huge circle above the majestic falls! American — Bridal Veil — Horseshoe — all are visible in one awed glance. In perfect safety you sail far above one of the Seven Modern Wonders of the World — looking down from the windowed cabin of another modern wonder — the airplane."

The 1927 brochure shows an S-38 Sikorsky amphibian.

One-way fare was $17.50 in either direction.

TAC's Keystone-Loening Air Yachts carried six passengers, together with 500 lbs of baggage, mail and express. TAC started this over-water service in 1929. In 1931 the airline name was changed to Transamerican Airlines Corp.

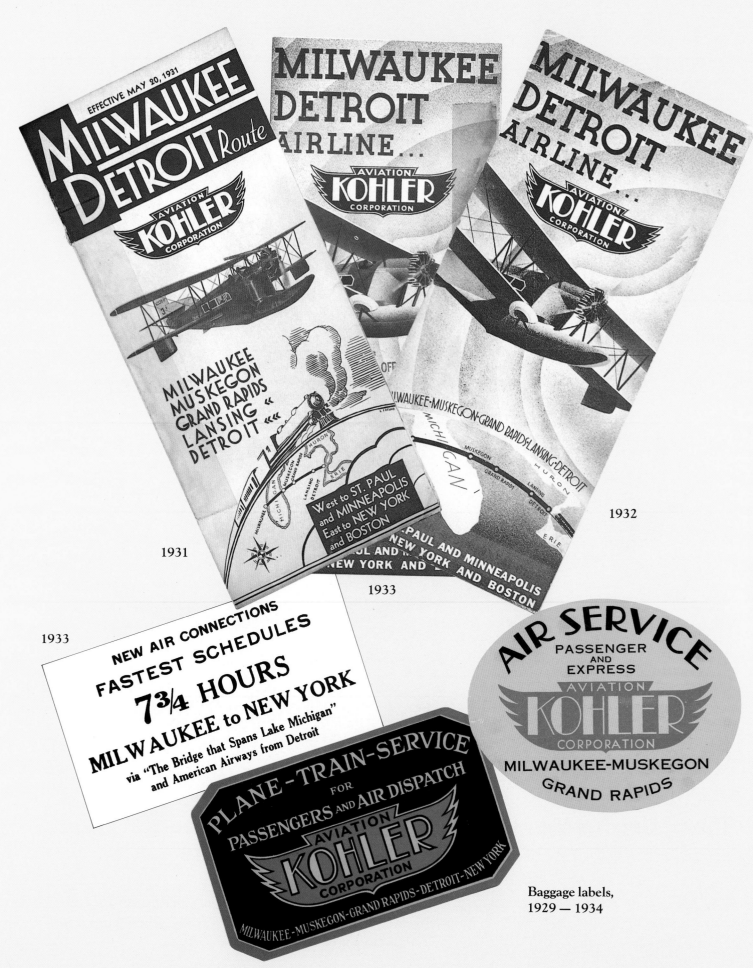

1931

1933

1932

1933

Baggage labels,
1929 — 1934

A PAA subsidiary.

COAST to COAST via PAA!

Twice daily service with Ford trimotors.

In 1937 this was the fastest coast-to-coast service in North America. (The route was only 50 miles long.)

A predecessor, ISTHMIAN AIRWAYS, ran the same service, starting in 1929. They used five all-metal Hamilton seaplanes which could carry eight passengers.

Antilles Air Boats: Timetable

SEAPLANE AIRLINE

The Goose

WORLD'S LARGEST

Linking Downtown
St. Thomas
St. Croix
St. John
St. Martin
Tortola
Fajardo
San Juan

1973 timetable

This airline was organized by Charles Blair, who flew the VS-44A flying boats for American Export Lines, and later flew with American Overseas Airlines and Pan American Airways. He capped his love for these big 4-engined boats by buying and flying two Short Sandringham Empire flying boats from Australia to the Virgin Islands. One of these was chartered by Aer Arann to use on the Irish lakes in the summer time, but neither was successful in obtaining permits from the U.S. air authorities to use on scheduled services. Blair was drowned in an unfortunate landing in heavy seas by one of the Grumman Gooses. (They were never called Geese).

Grumman Goose

Grumman Mallard

The VS-44A "Excambion" was bought from Catalina Air Lines in 1967 and renamed "Excalibur VII." Hull damage eventually forced this "Mother Goose" to retire. It is presently being restored at the Sikorsky plant in Connecticut. It is the only 4-engine American-made commercial flying boat still in existence and will be exhibited at the New England Air Museum.

**Short Sandringham "Excalibur VIII,"
formerly "Islander" of Ansett Airlines.**

**VS-44A "Excambion," renamed
"Excalibur VII" by Blair.**

CHALK'S

The Oldest Airline in the World
WITH 55 YEARS OF CONTINUOUS SERVICE

NASSAU — BAHAMAS — BIMINI

Daily Flights to Bimini
With Additional Service on Weekends

Daily scheduled non-stop flights between downtown Miami and downtown Nassau in the Bahamas.

With Customs and Immigration
at our private terminals there is no delay.

Tickets from other U.S. carriers are accepted.

WATCH THE CHANGING COLORS OF THE BAHAMIAN WATERS AND THE BIG FISH SUNNING THEMSELVES ON THE SAND FLATS.

Free parking within 50 feet of the plane at both terminals.

How Many Times Do You Get the Chance to Experience the Safety and Fun of a Seaplane AT THE SAME PRICE AS A JET.

For reservations call:
(305) 377-8801
MacArthur Causeway — Miami, Fla.
in Nassau 52845

CHALK'S predated KLM and SCADTA by a few months in 1919 to claim to be the world's oldest airline still flying, but Chalk's has its own definition for such a claim, which might not survive a close examination. Route is from Miami to the Bahamas with Grumman seaplanes.

Propaganda sticker

VIRGIN ISLANDS SEAPLANE SHUTTLE took over ANTILLES AIRBOATS' fleet of Mallards and its Virgin Islands routes.

Baggage sticker

中國航空公司
China National Aviation Corp.

滬粵綫
SHANGHAI-CANTON LINE

飛航時刻及客票價目表
Time Tables & Passenger Fare Rates

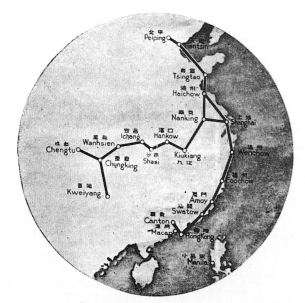

C. N. A. C. Air Routes.

二十五年十二月十日起實行   Corrected to December 10, 1936

中國航空公司
航空載運旅客郵件
AIRMAIL & PASSENGER SERVICE
Name
From   To
No
Date
CHINA NATIONAL AVIATION CORP.

CHINA NATIONAL AVIATION CORP

A 1936 timetable and CNAC's earliest baggage label, which pictures their first type of aircraft, a Loening amphibian.

The Douglas Dolphin was used on the Shanghai-Canton line.

The Shanghai-Peiping line operated five days a week with Stinsons and two days with Douglas DC-2s.

On the Shanghai-Chengtu line DC-2s and Ford Tr-Motors were used from Shanghai to Hankow. From Hankow to Chungking Loenings were employed. From Chungking to Chengtu a Stinson was used, and from Chungking to Kweiyang a Ford.

In 1933 Pan American Airways bought the Curtiss-Keys interest in CNAC, and by 1937 had added a Sikorsky S-43 to the fleet.

The Douglas Dolphin.
This timetable all in Chinese.

This 1930 brochure shows the two S-38 Sikorsky amphibians which INTER-ISLAND AIRWAYS operated between the main islands of Hawaii.

In 1941 their name was changed to HAWAIIAN AIRLINES.

Inside their 1931 timetable.

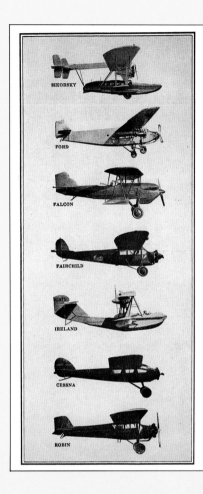

"The world's oldest flying organization". A July 15, 1929, leaflet, centerfold of which is shown above, boasts of 18 years of air transportation experience.

The Sikorsky cabin amphibion is described as a "giant twin-engined craft" and could be chartered at $1.60 per mile. Capacity was 8 passengers.

The Ireland was available as an open cockpit flying boat of 70¢ per mile or as a cabin amphibion at 75¢ per mile. Capacity was four passengers.

By 1930 the merger of CURTISS and WRIGHT was apparent. All the many brochures now used the name CURTISS-WRIGHT on front, as shown on right, rather than CURTISS alone, as on the brochure at left. Right: A Loening amphibian.

554:—Up-To-Date Transportation Between Catalina Island and Mainland.

In the early 1920s PACIFIC MARINE AIRWAYS operated two Curtiss HS2L flying boats in the Los Angeles to Catalina Island service. Fare was $12.50 one-way.

In 1928 the company was bought by WESTERN AIR EXPRESS, who operated the route until 1931, when WILMINGTON-CATALINA AIRLINES took over.

WESTERN AIR EXPRESS's 1928 brochure is shown at right. The S-38 Sikorsky amphibians were being used, and a fare reduction was in effect. ($10).

A "giant Sikorsky land and water plane" — a "mammoth airliner," a "sesqui-plane," it says inside. (It carried 8 passengers.)

In 1931 WILMINGTON-CATALINA AIRLINE took over the Catalina flights from WESTERN AIR EXPRESS, replacing the Loening amphibians with Douglas Dolphins. By 1937 fares were down to $5. One-way. Service ceased in 1942 due to wartime restrictions.

Fly to . . .
Catalina Island
VIA
NEW
Flying Boat
SERVICE

— IN —
LUXURY and COMFORT

AVALON AIR TRANSPORT
PACIFIC LANDING
FOOT OF LONG BEACH FREEWAY
LONG BEACH HARBOR, CALIFORNIA
HEmlock 6-9756 · NEvada 6-6500

CATALINA ISLAND BY AIR

just 15 min

catalina air lines, inc.

YOU ARE THERE IN LESS THAN TWENTY MINUTES!

"ASK ME ANOTHER"

It has been the experience of the **Wilmington-Catalina Airline** that the public traveling by air asks many questions. To assist in the answering of these questions this small folder has been prepared. We would appreciate any suggestions that you have to offer and trust that you enjoy your trip to the utmost.

* * *

In 1935 AVALON AIR TRANSPORT began operations to Catalina Island from Long Beach. Grumman Goose amphibians were being used by 1953. In 1957 the Sikorsky VS-44A flying boat "Excambion" was bought and added to the fleet of Gooses. In 1963 the company name was changed to CATALINA AIR LINES INC. The big flying boat continued to operate until 1967 when it was sold to ANTILLES AIR BOATS in the U.S. Virgin Islands.

In the 1970s and 1980s more than one small airline continues the flying boat services to Catalina Island. (left)

Baggage label

59

1930's

In the early 1930s air express to Latin America was started. The S-40, largest aircraft in use at the time, is shown.

This brochure states "There is no article in foreign trade, with the single exception of heavy livestock, which Pan American has not carried."

Miami to Havana — "2 hours".
Miami to Buenos Aires — "7 days".

Airmail was a much-needed service and also a profitable cargo for PAA.

Small stickers in English, Spanish and Portuguese were widely used to advertise the express service to Latin America.

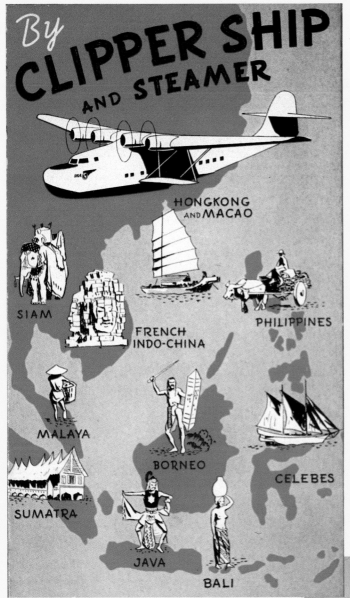

This little folder advertises tours to Southeast Asia via the Transpacific "China Clipper" types, then by rail, motor, or steamship to many destinations in the Dutch East Indies, French Indo-China, Siam, Malaya, and the Philippines. A 24-day tour from Singapore to Java and Bali is offered, with extension to Sumatra.

This is one of the shorter tours offered. Two steamship lines are used as well as motor and rail thru Java. Travel in the Far East in those days was time-consuming. The Clippers were instrumental in introducing faster travel by air to many of these remote destinations. Most other travel took weeks instead of days.

Here is a later pitch for flying vacations. This long PAA foldout has pages for: "GO AIR CRUISING TO MEXICO-GUATEMALA"; "WING AWAY TO THE WEST INDIES"; "BERMUDA 5 HOURS BY CLIPPER"; "ALASKA BY AIR"; "TO HISTORIC PERU OR DAZZLING RIO"; and "SEE ALL SOUTH AMERICA BY AIR". "How long?", "How much?", and "When?" are all explained in detail.

About the Author and Photographer:

Don Thomas has spent a lifetime in radio communications, including 13 years in the Merchant Marine as Radio Officer on Transatlantic liners, tankers, freighters, fishing trawlers and cruise liners. He worked for three broadcast stations, for RCA and for Eastern Airlines. He then spent several years with Tropical Radio (United Fruit) in Florida and Central America. In 1942 he started ferrying two-engined lend-lease bombers as a radio-navigator for PAA Ferries from Miami across the South Atlantic to the Russians in Iran and the RAF in Cairo. On his last flight for PAAF in a PBY5A amphibian the plane cracked up on take off in Eritrea. After the airforce took over ferrying of all aircraft late in 1942 he was commissioned in the Naval Reserve and trained flight radio operators at NAS Alameda and air navigators at NAS Pensacola. Before the war ended he was back in the Merchant Marine on convoy trips to Europe. After the war he joined the U.S. Foreign Service and served in 10 countries before retiring. Twice a widower, he now raises tropical birds, collects butterflies in tropical countries, and continues writing and collecting historic aviation and steamship timetables, brochures, postcards and baggage labels.

Many thanks to Winston Williams
for advice and assistance in photography.

Additional copies of this book may be ordered at $16.00 plus $1 for postage and packing from:

Don Thomas
1801 Oak Creek Drive
Dunedin, FL 34698.